THE Complete
Church
Clip Art Book

by Rick Bundschuh

with the additional talents of

Tom Finley
Brad McLeod
and
Warren Dayton

STANDARD
PUBLISHING
Cincinnati, Ohio

Contents

Introduction

Introduction

You don't have to be an artist to produce great-looking documents. In fact, using the art in this book, you can create T-shirts, stationery, overhead transparencies, book covers; the limit is your imagination.

Tools You Will Need

1. Scissors
2. Rubber Cement
3. Cellophane tape
4. Correction fluid
5. A 90-degree, clear triangle
6. Black felt-tip pens of various thicknesses
7. A metal-edge ruler
8. A pencil and eraser
9. A light blue (non-reproductive) pencil

Other helpful tools are a T-square, a single-edged razor blade or an X-Acto knife (a #11 blade is best), and a good working surface, such as a drawing board.

Some Helpful Hints

There are two basic ways to use a collection of clip art. One is to have an idea for your printed material and look for the perfect piece of art to illustrate it. The other is to look through the collection and let a piece of art suggest an idea to you. The second way is usually the least frustrating, but after you are familiar with the art in this book, you will be able to locate pieces that you know it contains.

Before you begin cutting this book apart, you may wish to devise a method for filing the pieces removed for possible reuse. Probably the least troublesome way of saving the pieces (and the book) is to photocopy the page containing the piece you wish to use, and use the photocopy as your original art. That way, you need never cut into the book.

The second least troublesome way to save all the art is to replace each piece in the exact spot from which you removed it. Leave borders of the book pages intact—never cut from the edge of the page into a piece of art! If you do, you will soon have all sorts of scraps sticking out of your book that will get wrinkled or torn off, and then you will not have a hole to receive the returned art.

When you find the piece of art you want to use, place something you don't mind cutting into behind the page and use your razor blade or X-Acto knife to cut through the white space around the art. Do not try to cut on the outline of the art, and be careful not to cut into adjoining pieces. Lift your art from the hole you have created, and when you are finished with it, replace it in the same hole. Tape the art lightly in place <u>on the back of the art;</u> never place tape over lines of the art. Masking tape is good for this job as it is easily removed, or you may simply cut through cellophane tape when you need the piece again.

It is usually a good idea to find your piece of art before writing the copy that will accompany it, not only so that the two will work together, but also because the size of the art may dictate how much space is left for copy (if you don't have a copy machine that reduces or enlarges).

There are generally two sizes of each piece of art in this book, but if neither size is exactly what you want, you'll need to reduce or enlarge it. Keep in mind that when art is slightly reduced, it tends to have a cleaner, sharper image, and art that is <u>greatly</u> enlarged may have fuzzy edges or be somewhat distorted. If you do not have access to a photocopy machine that reduces and/or enlarges, many print ships will do this for a minimal cost. In

fact, if you are producing a piece that requires a professional look, you may also want to have your copy set in type (typeset) at a print shop. In this case, you many indicate the area you want the art to fill, the areas you want your headline and copy to fill, and either work with the printer to design your piece, or let the printer do it for you. With the advent of desktop publishing equipment, these services are becoming more and more reasonable in price.

For do-it-yourself jobs, you may want to invest in some of the hundreds of attractive type styles in hundreds of sizes that are available in rub-on or cutout letters. Check your local art or office supply stores for brands such as Letraset and FORMATT. Another acceptable way to produce headlines, especially if you do have an artistic flair, is to hand-letter the words. For more on how to do this, see "Preparing the Paste-Up."

Also available from art or office supply stores are rub-on screens for adding color to posters and overhead transparencies, or skin tones and dramatic shading to reproducible items. For example, if you need a piece of art that depicts a multi-racial group, simply place screens of varying degrees of darkness over the clip art figures, rub into place, and cut around the edges with your razor or knife.

Preparing a Dummy and/or a Paste-Up

If you are turning in hand-written (not a good idea!) or typed material to a printer to be typeset, a "dummy" need be nothing more than a pencil sketch of the layout (where you want everything to go) of your final product. Be sure to double check your spelling and accuracy of information before delivering it to the printer, or before typing your final copy yourself. If you are doing the typing, use an electric typewriter so that all the letters will have the same weight, and use a carbon ribbon, if possible, for the best reproduction. When you are preparing the final piece that will be photocopied or printed, your "paste-up" must be more exact.

As you plan where your art and copy is to go on the page, make sure to leave <u>at least</u> a 1/2" margin all around the page. This will keep your art and copy from running or "bleeding" off the edge of the page, and will also help to keep the page from looking cramped. The obvious exception is if you <u>want</u> a piece of art to run off the edge of a page. This can be a design device to capture attention, encourage a viewer to turn the page, or simply be funny.

If you are preparing a paste-up, use your triangle to set the lines of copy down straight, or at such an angle that it is obviously not a mistake. (See the title page of this book.)

Portions of copy that you want to highlight within the body of the article can be underlined, set in bold type, a larger type size, or can be surrounded with a box. Be sure to identify such requests before delivering your copy to a printer. Once your art and copy (either typeset or typed) is temporarily in place, you'll know how much room you have for a headline. If you have not had this headline set by the printer, now is the time to get out your rub-on letters or hand-letter the headline.

<u>First,</u> check the spelling and accuracy of your information. Nothing is more frustrating than carefully preparing a headline only to discover that you've given the wrong date, or misspelled a word! Next, if you're using rub-on letters, carefully read the directions in the package. They will contain many time-saving and how-to tips. If you are hand-lettering the headline, use your non-reproducible blue pencil to sketch in the placement of the letters. When the spacing, size, and shape of the letters pleases you, have someone else check the spelling again. When you work closely over a project for some time, you can fail to see the most obvious mistakes! Now go over your blue pencil with a dark (black is best) felt-tip pen. If your pen "bleeds" (you get fuzzy edges), you can either outline these letters with a black ball-point pen, (be careful not to create grooves in the paper) or start over on a heavier, smoother type of paper. (Tip: check to see if your pen bleeds on the paper <u>before</u> you do all the lettering!)

It may take you several tries to get a headline that you are pleased with. Once you have it, <u>that</u> piece of paper may be cut apart and treated as a piece of art, or it may become the background for the rest of your pieces.

Now your art and copy (either typeset or typed) may be pasted in place using rubber cement. You can lift and reposition your papers before it dries, or even after, if you follow the directions on the bottle. Excess rubber cement can be rubbed away after a few minutes of drying time.

To avoid the black "cutlines" that can appear on your printed or photocopied sheet, use transparent tape or a new product called "Tack A Note" (from Dennison) along the edges of your artwork. Make sure your hands are clean since the tape will pick up and transfer fingerprints and smudges to the art. Rub, or burnish, the tape for a secure fit.

Check your page carefully for pencil lines, ink smudges, or fingerprints. Erase these or cover them with correction fluid, then on to the copy machine!

8 Sports Activities and Youth Stuff

Chapter 1: Sports Activities and Youth Stuff

10 Sports Activities and Youth Stuff

12 Sports Activities and Youth Stuff

SENIOR
HIGH

JUNIOR
HIGH

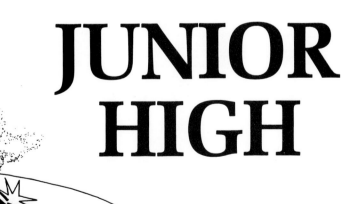

14 Sports Activities and Youth Stuff

SKATE PARTY

SKATE PARTY

SKATE PARTY · SKATE PARTY · SKATE PARTY · SKATE PARTY

16 Sports Activities and Youth Stuff

18 Sports Activities and Youth Stuff

BIKE HIKE

MINIATURE GOLF

BIKE HIKE

MINIATURE GOLF

MINIATURE GOLF

20 Sports Activities and Youth Stuff

SLUMBER PARTY

SLUMBER PARTY

22 Sports Activities and Youth Stuff

24 Sports Activities and Youth Stuff

BANANA
SPLIT

HAPPY
BIRTHDAY

30 Sports Activities and Youth Stuff

MADNESS

SELF IMAGE

SELF IMAGE

32 Sports Activities and Youth Stuff

PRIMARY

JUNIOR

MIDDLER

34 Sports Activities and Youth Stuff

36 Sports Activities and Youth Stuff

CAMPOUT

38 Sports Activities and Youth Stuff

40 Sports Activities and Youth Stuff

42 Sports Activities and Youth Stuff

46 Sports Activities and Youth Stuff

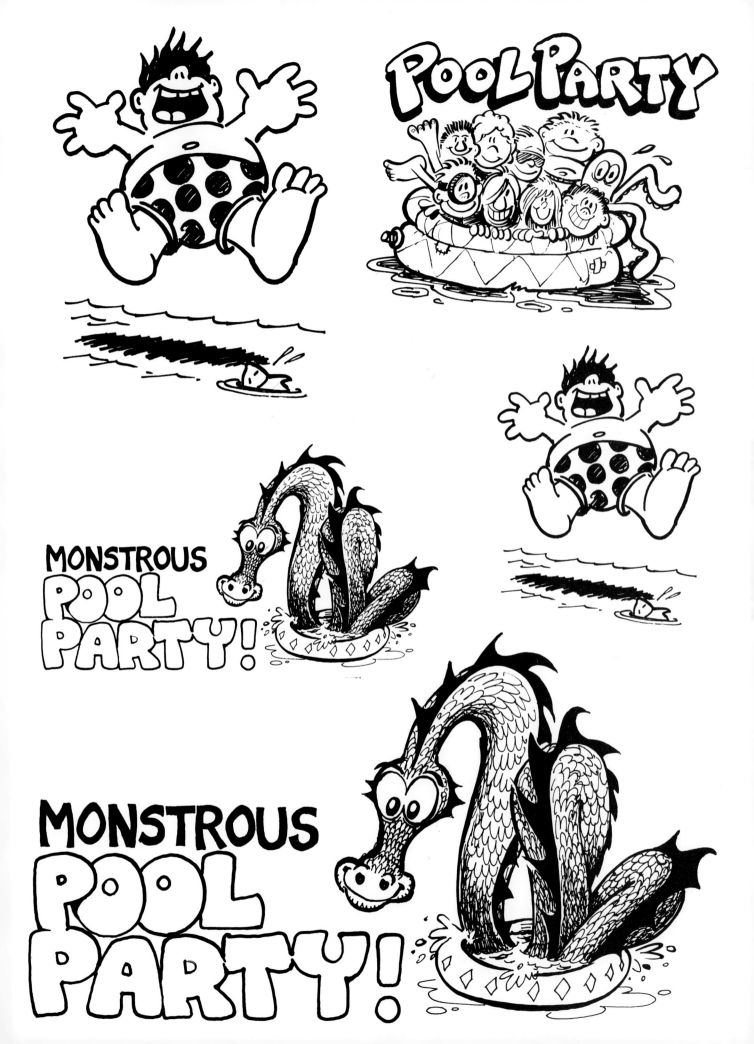

POOL PARTY

MONSTROUS POOL PARTY!

MONSTROUS POOL PARTY!

48 Sports Activities and Youth Stuff

50 Sports Activities and Youth Stuff

56 Sports Activities and Youth Stuff

58 Sports Activities and Youth Stuff

60 Sports Activities and Youth Stuff

64 Sports Activities and Youth Stuff

66 Sports Activities and Youth Stuff

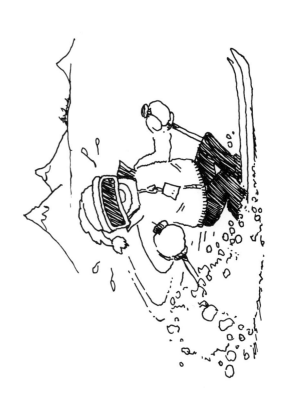

68 Sports Activities and Youth Stuff

70 Sports Activities and Youth Stuff

Chapter 2: Church Life

TAKE A LOOK IN THE BOOK

TAKE A LOOK IN THE BOOK

HIS·LOVE
SET·US
FREE

HIS·LOVE
SET·US
FREE

MAKE A JOYFUL NOISE UNTO THE LORD

MAKE A JOYFUL NOISE UNTO THE LORD

JESUS IS LORD

Your **Donations**
Are Welcomed

Your **Donations**
Are Welcomed

Pastor Appreciation Day

Pastor Appreciation Day

OUR BUILDING FUND COULD USE YOUR HELP!

HELP
NEEDED!!

Pastor Appreciation Day

Your *Donations* Are Welcomed

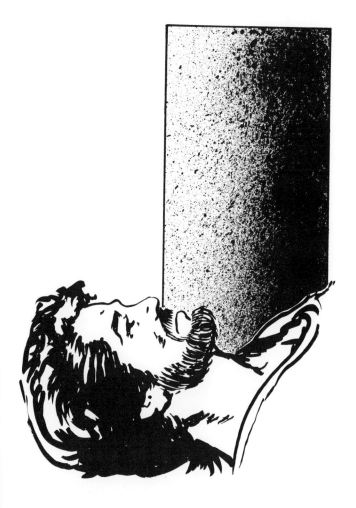

I WAS HOMELESS... AND YOU HOUSED ME

HELP NEEDED!!

I WAS HOMELESS... AND YOU HOUSED ME

I WAS HOMELESS... AND YOU HOUSED ME

OUR BUILDING FUND COULD USE YOUR HELP!

COOKOUT

Round-up

Round-up

CAR WASH

BAKE SALE

PANCAKE SUPPER

BREAKFAST

MUSICAL

CANTATA
MUSICAL

CHOIR
PRACTICE

O WHAT WONDROUS LOVE

O WHAT WONDROUS LOVE

BIBLE

BIBLE

BIBLE

BIBLE

GO....

INTO ALL THE WORLD

MISSIONS
MISSIONS WEEK
MISSIONS SUNDAY

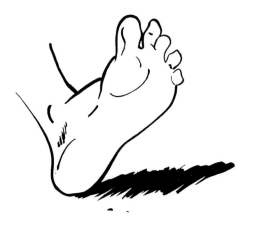

Go into all the world

WORKDAY

WE COULD
USE SOME
EXTRA HANDS

WE COULD
USE SOME
EXTRA HANDS

CHURCH CLEAN-UP DAY

CHURCH CLEAN-UP DAY

NURSERY
TODDLERS

2's and 3's

4's and 5's

GRAB A FRIEND (OR TWO)

GRAB A FRIEND (OR TWO)

MOTHER'S DAY

MOTHER/DAUGHTER

EARLY CHILDHOOD

FOR KIDS ONLY

CHOMP

COOKIES

Girls Only

KID STUFF

EASTER SERVICE

4TH OF JULY

PICNIC
4th OF JULY

4TH OF JULY

Come ye thankful people

We gather together to ask the Lord's blessing

THANKSGIVING

HAPPY THANKSGIVING

We gather together to ask the Lord's blessing

Give Thanks

Give Thanks

BURP!

MERRY CHRISTMAS

A Child Is Born
A Son Is Given

A Child Is Born
A Son Is Given

Peace On Earth

Peace On Earth

CANDLELIGHT SERVICE

CANDLELIGHT SERVICE

MERRY CHRISTMAS

JESUS
THE REASON
FOR THE SEASON

JESUS
THE REASON
FOR THE SEASON

Christ the Savior is born!

Christ the Savior is born!

Chapter 5: Notices, Borders, Forms, etc.

190 Notices, Borders, and Forms

192 Notices, Borders, and Forms

200 Notices, Borders, and Forms

202 Notices, Borders, and Forms

REMEMBER IN PRAYER
PRAYER REQUEST

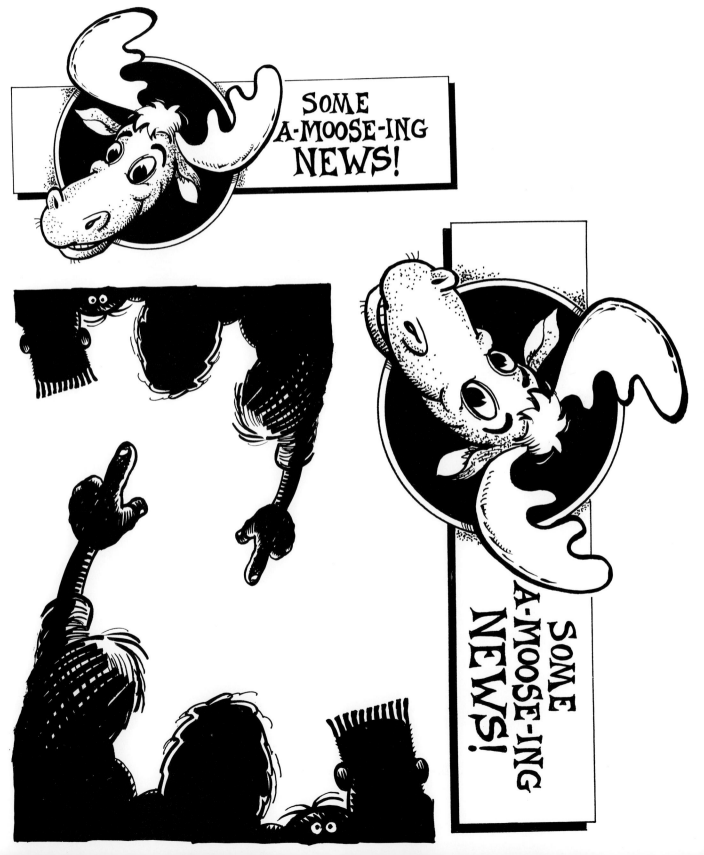

204 Notices, Borders, and Forms

FLASH!

FLASH!

**NEWS
REPORT**

HELP NEEDED!!

210 Notices, Borders, and Forms

Surprise Party

PLEASE EAT THIS INVITATION AFTER READING !!!

 FOR:

 WHEN:

 WHERE:

AND PLEASE... KEEP YOUR MOUTH SHUT.!!

212 Notices, Borders, and Forms

Sunday School

Open House

Date _____

Time _____

Place _____

Sermon Notes

214 Notices, Borders, and Forms

Youth Group
Phone
Directory

Phone
Directory

216 Notices, Borders, and Forms

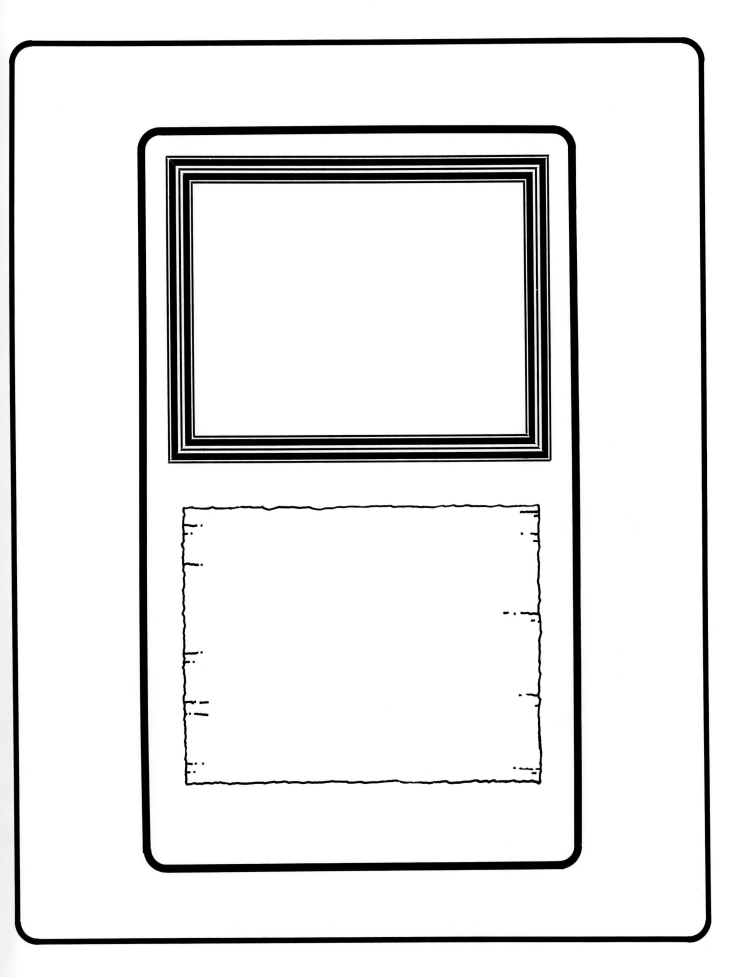

Certificate of Achievement

Awarded To

220 Notices, Borders, and Forms

GREETINGS!

Just a note...

Teacher's Meeting

224 Notices, Borders, and Forms

NOTE

Coming Up...

228 Notices, Borders, and Forms

SIGN UP LIST

Event_____Date_____Cost_____

Time _____ Bring _____

Name	Phone
1.	
2.	
3.	
4.	
5.	
6.	
7.	
8.	
9.	
10.	
11.	
12.	
13.	
14.	
15.	
16.	
17.	
18.	
19.	
20.	

230 Notices, Borders, and Forms

Medical Release Form

Name _____

Address _____

Phone _____

Person to contact in case of emergency: _____

Home Phone _____ Bus. Phone _____

Birthdate _____

In case we cannot be reached during an Emergency, I (we) the undersigned give permission for our child to be treated by a licensed physician, and for said physician to administer whatever care is necessary, including anesthesia, for their safety and care.

Signed _____ Date _____

(Parent or Guardian)

Please note any medical allergies, medical problems, medications being taken or other information that is pertinent:

_____

_____

Medical Release Form

Name _____

Address _____

Phone _____

Person to contact in case of emergency: _____

Home Phone _____ Bus. Phone _____

Birthdate _____

In case we cannot be reached during an Emergency, I (we) the undersigned give permission for our child to be treated by a licensed physician, and for said physician to administer whatever care is necessary, including anesthesia, for their safety and care.

Signed _____ Date _____

(Parent or Guardian)

Please note any medical allergies, medical problems, medications being taken or other information that is pertinent:

_____

_____

Medical Release Form

Name _____

Address _____

Phone _____

Person to contact in case of emergency: _____

Home Phone _____ Bus. Phone _____

Birthdate _____

In case we cannot be reached during an Emergency, I (we) the undersigned give permission for our child to be treated by a licensed physician, and for said physician to administer whatever care is necessary, including anesthesia, for their safety and care.

Signed _____ Date _____

(Parent or Guardian)

Please note any medical allergies, medical problems, medications being taken or other information that is pertinent:

_____

_____

Medical Release Form

Name _____

Address _____

Phone _____

Person to contact in case of emergency: _____

Home Phone _____ Bus. Phone _____

Birthdate _____

In case we cannot be reached during an Emergency, I (we) the undersigned give permission for our child to be treated by a licensed physician, and for said physician to administer whatever care is necessary, including anesthesia, for their safety and care.

Signed _____ Date _____

(Parent or Guardian)

Please note any medical allergies, medical problems, medications being taken or other information that is pertinent:

_____

_____

232 Notices, Borders, and Forms

Sat.				
Fri.				
Thurs.				
Wed.				
Tues.				
Mon.				
Sun.				

234 Notices, Borders, and Forms

JANUARY	MONDAY	6:00
FEBRUARY	TUESDAY	6:30
MARCH	WEDNESDAY	7:00
APRIL	THURSDAY	7:30
MAY	FRIDAY	8:00
JUNE	SATURDAY	8:30
JULY	SUNDAY	9:00
AUGUST	MON.	9:30
SEPTEMBER	TUES.	AM
OCTOBER	WED.	PM
NOVEMBER	THURS.	a.m.
DECEMBER	FRI.	p.m.

6:00	a.m.	8:00
6:30	p.m.	8:30
7:00	AM	9:00
7:30	PM	9:30

HAPPY
NEW
YEAR
HARVEST
FESTIVAL
MERRY
CHRISTMAS
CHRISTMAS
EVE
SERVICE
EASTER
SUNRISE SERVICE

MEMORIAL DAY

VICTORIA DAY

CANADA DAY

ASH
WEDNESDAY

GOOD FRIDAY

ELDERS PROMOTION SUNDAY
DEACONS COLLEGE/CAREER
TRUSTEES PRAYER MEETING
MEETING BOARD MEETING
DISCIPLESHIP C.E. COMMITTEE
ANNIVERSARY STAFF MEETING
JUST MARRIED TEACHERS
GUEST SPEAKER MEETING
RUMMAGE SALE BUILDING
NEW ADDITIONS COMMITTEE
CHOIR PRACTICE MEMBERSHIP
GUEST MUSICIAN COMMITTEE
SENIOR CITIZENS MEETING
YOUNG MARRIEDS BANQUET
CONGRATULATIONS BAPTISM
CHURCH MEMBERSHIP SINGLES
POTLUCK CARRY-IN DINNER
NEW MEMBERS CLASS NEWS
BABY CHILD DEDICATION DAY